Tell, Tale Signs Of Spring!

SPRINGTIME WEATHER IS WARM.

YOU KNOW NOT TOO COLD AND, NOT TOO HOT.

TREE FLOWERS BLOOM ON MANY TREES.

WITH COLORS OF PINK, WHITE, PURPLE AND, even YELLOW!

Hmmmmmm.......
Tell, Tale signs of Spring!

BUMBLEBEES SNIFF ON FLOWERS, THAT SPRANG UP FROM THE GROUND.

AS YOU PASS BY, YOU CAN HEAR THE BZZZZZZZ....... SOUND.

MARCH, APRIL AND MAY
ARE SPRINGTIME MONTHS.

THAT WILL EACH BRING
A SURPRISE EVERY MONTH!

HMMMMMM.......
TELL, TALE SIGNS OF SPRING!

EGGS ARE COVERED IN PRETTY COLORS.

ON THE EASTER HOLIDAY,
LIKE NONE OTHER.

IN THE SPRINGTIME WE WEAR LIGHT CLOTHING SUCH AS, SHORT SLEEVE SHIRTS, SHORT PANTS AND SKIRTS.

AND WE ADORN OUR FEET
WITH OPEN TOE SHOES.

HOW'S THAT UNTIL WE CAN GET IN THE SWIMMING POOLS?

HMMMMMM.......
TELL, TALE SIGNS OF SPRING!

TICK, TOCK THE TIME GOES FORWARD.

OH, THE DAYS WILL BE LONGER;
LET'S HOPE WE DON'T GET BORED.

SPRING COMES IN BETWEEN
WINTER AND SUMMER.

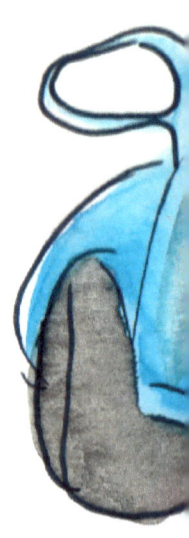

THAT SHOULD BE A STICKER FOR A CAR'S BUMPER!

SPRING GARDENING BRINGS SOME PEOPLE JOY; I BELIEVE.

BUT, FIRST THEY HAVE TO GET THE SOIL RIGHT FROM THE WINTER DEBRIS.

Hmmmmm........
Tell, Tale Signs of Spring!

REMEMBER, SPRINGTIME IS
A BEAUTIFUL SCENE AND THOSE FLOWERS
WILL MAKE YOU SING!

www.ingramcontent.com/pod-product-compliance
Lightning Source LLC
Chambersburg PA
CBHW041536280526
45792CB00004B/1519